NORWICH OVER THE WATER:
demolition and change

The northern city centre before and during redevelopment 1965-73

Edited by Matthew Williams

© Matthew Williams

First published 2020 by Independent Publishing Network.

Distributed by SCT Books, 75 Christchurch Road, Norwich NR2 3NG.
info@smartcycletraining.co.uk

All rights reserved. No portion of this publication may be reproduced, copied or transmitted except with written permission or in accordance with the provisions of the Copyright, Designs and Patents Act 1988, or under the terms of any licence permitting limited copying issued by the Copyright Licensing Agency, Saffron House, 6-10 Kirby Street, London EC1N 8TS.

ISBN 978-1-78972-841-5

Typset in MS Calibri and Times New Roman by SCT Books

Manufactured in the UK by Imprint Digital, Exeter

Front cover illustration: Rear view of 67 Pitt Street during demolition in June 1973 (Jess Lince collection)

Rear cover illustration: Calvert Street Methodist Chapel as pictured in March 1936 (George Plunkett collection), and during its demolition in August 1966 (Mike Adcock collection)

Contents

Pre-1965 map showing photo locations *inside front cover*

Introduction 1

Acknowledgements 6

Photographs 1-193 (monochrome) 8

Colour plates *after monochrome photographs*

Index to numbered photographs *at end of book*

Post-1973 map showing photo locations *inside rear cover*

Introduction

For several centuries, the northern part of Norwich city centre, known as Norwich Over the Water, was the industrial engine room of the city. By the 1960s, it had become obvious it was on borrowed time.

For a long time, there had been many factories interspersed with blocks of densely-packed houses, often arranged in yards, where the workers and their families lived. But as the unsettled years of the twentieth century rolled on, things were changing. Manufacturing was moving away out of old cramped premises and local residents had transferred into more aspirational accommodation in the growing suburbs beyond the city centre.

A combination of ongoing slum clearance and mass demolition ahead of the construction of the inner ring road and Anglia Square left parts of the area as urban wasteland. During the 1960s there appeared many unpaved open spaces which became used for indiscriminate car parking for local workers amongst the remaining heaps of rubble. In time, new housing development and the processes of gentrification would begin to mend the scars, but some such areas still remain at the time of writing.

An example is the space between Pitt Street and St George's Street, originally earmarked for another wing of the Anglia Square complex, but stubbornly persisting for 50 years as an apparently abandoned, largely vacant patch. The site is still flanked by a pile of rubble containing some of the crushed remains of the buildings that once stood there. Many of those will have had cellars that may still exist beneath the rough ground surface, coarsely infilled with debris.

The incongruous way in which the inner ring road was bulldozed across the medieval street pattern, at an angle to the natural 'grain' of the city, left numerous irregularly-shaped fragments of land along its wake. It is not surprising that these now meaningless pieces of urban space, bounded as they are by buildings or highway from which there is no ready access, have failed to find productive use. The sterilising effect on adjacent land meant that the corridor devoured by the new road was rather more than the 20 metres width taken for the dual carriageway itself, expanding to more than 50 metres in the vicinity of St Crispin's roundabout - some of which blighted land remains to this day simply overgrown with brambles.

Anglia Square itself was constructed slightly later than the inner ring road. Its footprint, measuring almost 200 metres north to south and east to west, covers what had been a tightly-packed area of buildings and yards - a microcosm of urban activity for centuries. As soon as the development had been planned, the writing was on the wall: individual properties or blocks of buildings were gradually acquired, vacated, boarded up and knocked down. That fine urban texture was thus progressively wiped clear to allow for unfettered redevelopment.

It was doubtless argued at the time that some of the older buildings so unceremoniously demolished were in any case beyond economic repair after war damage, or had otherwise reached the end of their useful life. That cannot be said of the more modern edifices such as St Crispin's Hall (built in 1939) or certain older but well cared-for cultural gems such as Calvert

Street Methodist Chapel (built in 1810). Both simply stood in the way of the new road and had to go.

The demolitions for the inner ring road and Anglia Square in the 1960s were not of course the only site clearances within Norwich Over the Water – merely the culmination of a process that had started in the 1930s, under the guise of various improvement schemes.

Although these plans often spared particular buildings considered to be of architectural merit, an unfortunate side-effect of piecemeal clearance was to reduce the incentive for ongoing maintenance of the buildings that did survive. This accelerated a tendency for properties in the near vicinity to be allowed to become run-down, as can be observed in some of these photographs.

To understand what might be branded today as acts of civic vandalism, you have to appreciate the mindset of the planners and civic leaders of the time. In the difficult years after the Second World War, the desperate need was to rebuild a wounded city and to adopt a bold and forward-looking outlook – taking advantage of what was offered by modern building materials (notably reinforced concrete), new employment opportunities and the seemingly unlimited personal mobility offered by motor cars.

No longer was the improvement process just a matter of clearing away substandard housing and giving the people healthier places to live. Their daily lifestyles would also be transformed - by being able to travel further and faster, to shop in supermarkets and work in high-rise offices.

The decision-makers were not so blind as not to see that it would be necessary to sacrifice one or two cherished buildings to achieve this new infrastructure: that was unfortunate, but a poverty-stricken part of the city was being offered a new start with a clean slate. It was genuinely believed the modernisation plans were for the good of the populace - who could move out if they wished, or would no doubt soon learn to adjust if they chose to stay.

Nevertheless, there were more than a few thoughtful people at the time who held deep reservations about the choice of route for the inner ring road and flyover, and said so. Those views were of course set aside; the brutal and 'necessary' planning decisions were pushed through - not least out of a fear that the promised regeneration offered by Anglia Square and the new government offices might not happen if the road were delayed.

We can at least be grateful that there were Norwich citizens who, though lamenting the widespread obliteration of centuries-old streetscapes, were prepared to commit onto film what was there before it entirely disappeared; and the photographic coverage suggests they knew instinctively that the character of areas surrounding the clearance sites would also be changed forever.

Printed in this book is a numbered selection of 193 black and white images and 12 colour photos which it is hoped contribute to the record of this period of change in Norwich Over the Water from the mid 1960s until the early 1970s.

Most of the pictures were taken from the **Lince collection**, a set of some 350 photographs acquired from Jess Lince; these were taken by her late brother-in-law Tony Brown, some with the assistance of Jess (after he had developed Parkinson's disease). While the coverage is impressive, it is perhaps not on quite the comprehensive scale of George Plunkett's famous collection dating from the 1930s, 1950s and later, but it does complement that set of pictures. And unlike Plunkett, neither the dates nor the precise locations of the Lince pictures were systematically recorded, necessitating quite a task sorting, identifying and ordering the whole collection.

We have (with permission) taken the liberty of inserting into the numbered sequence eight contemporary pictures taken from **other sources** than the Lince collection, for the sake of coherence and completeness. The intention has been to make it easier to follow a more-or-less continuous route through the area while leafing through the book. These additions include monochrome photographs by Weaver, George Swain and Geoffrey Goreham taken from the Picture Norfolk collection, plus one of George Plunkett's pictures, and these are identified in the acknowledgements section below.

To support the usefulness and interest of this publication, both now and in the future, the locations for all black and white photographs within the numbered sequence have been referenced onto two versions of a **map** of the northern city centre. The map inside the front cover depicts the city layout prior to the main upheaval of the late 1960s and early 1970s, and that inside the back cover shows the modern layout, notably with the imposition of the inner ring road and Anglia Square, plus some more recent roadways.

A simple **index** of street names referenced to the photograph numbers has also been included at the back of the book.

Following directly after the series of black and white pictures is a short section containing the twelve contemporary **colour views** - to remind us that the world of the past was not all monochrome. Most, but not all, of these colour shots are from the Lince collection. Their locations have not been individually marked on the maps, but the colour pictures have been cross-referenced to the nearest black-and-white photographs within the numbered sequence, so it should be straightforward to work out the precise viewpoints.

The book is intended to be used either for browsing or for specific reference. Enjoy your immersion in a familiar city, but take yourself back to what can now seem a rather distant time, half a century ago.

M Williams
December 2019

Acknowledgements

It was during the editor's participation in the research phase of the *Anglia Square–A Love Story* project in early 2019* that the idea and opportunity arose to make publicly available the collection of photographs known as the Lince collection, most of which will not have been published before.

Members of that research group gave valuable help and encouragement during the early process of identifying photographic locations and cataloguing the collection.

Special thanks must be expressed to the original custodians of the photographs, not least Jess Lince and subsequently Peter Salt, for their willingness to allow them to be presented in the present form.

* A collaboration by the community theatre group The Common Lot

To supplement the Lince photographs, seven monochrome images (taken by Weaver, Swain and Goreham, appearing as photo nos. 4, 10, 13, 16, 25, 61 and 159) were reproduced courtesy of Norfolk County Council Library and Information Service, with their usual reminder that thousands of images of Norfolk's unique history can be enjoyed at their website www.picture.norfolk.gov.uk.

The generosity of Jonathan Plunkett is acknowledged in allowing use of two of his late father George Plunkett's images (photo no.15, and the upper image on the back cover). These were taken from the collection available online at www.georgeplunkett.co.uk.

Thanks too are due to Barbara Miller for making it possible to use colour transparencies originally forming part of the Mike Adcock collection, including three images used here (two colour views of St Martin's Lane and the photograph of Calvert Street Chapel under demolition on the back cover).

The image of pre-demolition Chamberlin's factory in the colour section is a photograph courtesy of Stefan Muthesius, and has been coloured in by hand.

The editor wishes to express personal thanks to certain other people for assistance and encouragement in the preparation of this book: notably Clare Everitt, Stuart McLaren, Stuart McPherson, Trevor Nuthall and Amanda Williams.

The maps and short captions have been provided primarily for identification reasons, and any errors in street numbers, viewpoints, dates or other factual material are entirely the editor's – who would be pleased to make necessary corrections if and when the opportunity arises.

1 – City Station Bridge, built in 1882, looking from Barn Road towards Norwich Over the Water

2 – The view along Station Road towards the area cleared ahead of construction of the inner ring road

3 – View from the bridge near what is now the Barn Road roundabout towards part of the cleared City Station site, now occupied by the access to Marriott's Way and warehouses off Barker Street

4 – The junction of Station Road and Oak Street, with the Fellmonger public house opposite (built in 1938 to replace the Railway Arms)

5 – Similar view as picture 4, with the pub under demolition

6 – St Martin's Lane, viewed from its junction with Oak Street

7 – St Martin's Lane, 69, after demolition of the adjacent building

8 – View back towards Oak Street, showing 65 and 67 St Martin's Lane prior to demolition

9 – Hipperson's premises at 59 St Martin's Lane *(see also colour photos showing the buildings to the right hand side, 47-53)*

10 – View from St Martin's Lane past 37 into the roadway leading to Cooke's Hospital. Like the parallel Quaker Lane to the Gildencroft Meeting House, this was shortly to be severed by the inner ring road

11 – Eastward view past 11 St Martin's Lane towards Pitt Street, with St Crispin's Hall visible in the distance

12 – Originally a fine Georgian house at 9 St Martin's Lane

13 – Looking towards the junction of St Martin's Lane with Pitt Street, with the south side of the road already cleared for the new road

14 - Looking back down St Martin's Lane, with the arched access to Butcher's Square on the right hand side

15 – St Crispin's Hall, opened in September 1939, as photographed by George Plunkett in May 1967 and demolished not long afterwards

16 – Awaiting demolition, the Flower in Hand public house in Pitt Street – now it would be standing in the middle of the road outside the office block - which still survives in 2019 in a refurbished form

17 – Looking from the same corner back out of town in the direction of St Augustine's – the building at the corner of Cherry Lane on the right is the former Cherry Tree public house - which has also survived to 2019 just north of Duke Street roundabout

18 – This section of St Crispin's Road between Pitt Street and St George's Street was constructed in 1937-8, but considerably widened in 1970-71

19 – This is a view of the rear of 134 St George's Street from the far side of St Crispin's Road, with a blank gable and boundary wall built when the adjacent house was removed for the road

20 – Northward view past St Crispin's Road and 134 St George's Street – note the road is still paved in granite sets

21 – Closer view of 134, with the opening to Cherry Lane beyond

22 – 134 St George's Street, looking back towards the city centre

23 – More modest houses on the opposite side of the road, further north at 97-103 St George's Street

24 – On the east side of St George's Street, 113-121

25 – Anchor Yard linked across from St George's Street to Calvert Street: this was about the last building between the two streets to be demolished

26 – Calvert Street Chapel celebrated its 150th anniversary in 1960 and was still going strong, before being compulsorily closed in June 1966 and knocked down later that year to make way for the inner ring road

27 – The high quality of the Georgian building was evident

28 – Calvert Street Chapel under demolition *(as back cover picture)*

29 – Shortly before its demolition, 76 Calvert Street on the west side

30 – Back to St George's Street, 71 and 73 stood opposite St Crispin's Road

31 – This former large house at 67 St George's Street was shown on later maps as a works

32 – Front door of 67 St George's Street

33 – Looking up St George's Street past 67 towards factory buildings

34 – View southwards past the Brush Factory building, which survives

35 – The former Kings Head inn at 63 St George's Street

36 – The Rifleman public house at 5 Cross Lane

37 – Former houses and latterly warehouse at 30-32 Calvert Street facing Golden Dog Lane *(see also colour photo)*

38 – Looking into Golden Dog Lane a few years before demolition

39 – A closer view of the old buildings at 15-19

40 – By the time of this photo, the old houses in Golden Dog Lane had been tidied up, but were then taken down not long afterwards

41 – Another view of 15-19 Golden Dog Lane *(see also colour photo)*

42 – Former weavers' premises to rear of 24 Magdalen Street

43 – Modern shop front, old building at 28 Magdalen Street, near to Golden Dog Lane

44 – View from St Saviour's Lane to the Magdalen Street junction

45 – This building at 47-49 Magdalen Street survived the construction of the flyover which replaced the buildings to the left

46 – All the buildings on the left half of this view (51 Magdalen Street onwards) were removed to accommodate the flyover

47 – The west side of the street showing 60-66 Magdalen Street, which were all subsequently taken down, with Botolph Street beyond

48 – Rear of 62 Magdalen Street, formerly part of Elephant Yard

49 – View back towards St Saviour's Church from near the junction of Botolph Street and Magdalen Street at Stump Cross

50 – These buildings at 51-53 Magdalen Street were lost, that on the right being the ancient Queen Victoria public house

51 – The magnificent Barclays Bank which stood at the Stump Cross forked junction between Botolph Street and Magdalen Street

52 – The flyover going in, occupying the space made by demolishing shops to the south of 68 Magdalen Street and 59 Magdalen Street

53 – The original view of 68 Magdalen Street and Botolph Street beyond, all of which buildings were eventually cleared

54 – Rear of the Queen Victoria public house before demolition, with a glimpse through the archway of Ling's Court across Magdalen Street to Elephant Yard

55 – Elevated view from the partially constructed inner ring road embankment towards St Saviour's Church

56 – The same viewpoint as for picture 57, but looking more towards the south across St Saviour's Lane to the factory building

57 – Looking further round towards the junction between St Saviour's Lane and Peacock Street, the severed part of which off Fishergate being subsequently renamed Blackfriars Street

58 – View from the severed Peacock Street towards St James's Church (a useful common visual reference point in this and the following two photos), with the flyover ramp nearing completion

59 - Similar view from the line of the inner ring road itself, with the truncated Barrack Street and the chimney of Steward & Patteson's brewery visible in the distance

60 – Looking eastwards into the original termination of Barrack Street at its junction with Peacock Street

61 – The same junction viewed in the opposite direction

62 – Looking southward down Cowgate towards Whitefriars Bridge, before the clearance of the buildings on the left, which fronted the original road line and occupied the site of the Carmelite Priory

63 – The ramp to the flyover is nearing completion - the new white gable ends are the two rows of terrace houses fronting Peacock Street and St Paul's Square, from which five houses were chopped off in each case

64 – Further up Magdalen Street from Stump Cross, here is Roys' former premises before it was replaced by a new store

65 – Almost opposite Roys, the Kummin Café and Radio Rentals shared what was a single building now numbered 82-84 Magdalen Street

66 – Roys at 79-85 Magdalen Street

67 – These buildings at 76-84 Magdalen Street were all subsequently covered by Anglia Square

68 – Dormer windows to 92-94 Magdalen Street

69 – This old building is now part of the Anglia Square sites. It stood almost opposite Cowgate, from which it is viewed here

70 – The south side of Cowgate, 6-12, one end of which survives

71 – The same buildings as in picture 70, from the opposite angle

72 – As in picture 69, with an ominous sign on the former factory wall at 100 Magdalen Street

73 – Former Hacon's Yard, to the rear of 92-94 Magdalen Street

74 – A closer view of the upper storeys at Hacon's Yard

75 – On the east side of the street facing the Mayfair Cinema, 113-117 Magdalen Street is now occupied by Secondhand Land

76 – Rear of 119-121 Magdalen Street

77 – Rear of 115-117 Magdalen Street

78 – A slightly later view of 115-117 Magdalen Street

79 – Looking northwards across the rear of properties at 113-119 Magdalen Street from Zipfel's Court

80 – Returning to 4-8 Botolph Street, this is the rear access to premises forming part of Frank Price's shop empire, from Cat and Fiddle Yard

81 – Rear of 14 Botolph Street

82 – Botolph Street, looking back towards Magdalen Street

83 – Old houses at 12-14 Botolph Street

84 – Access to Howlett's Court, viewed from the demolition site opposite 18 Botolph Street

85 – Frank Price's store formed much of the north side of the street

86 – Roberts Printing at 30-34 Botolph Street, formerly the clothing factory for Chamberlin's store built in 1903 *(see also coloured photo)*

87 – Boarded up awaiting demolition, the Kings Arms public house at the corner of Calvert Street

88 – The Kings Arms in Botolph Street, viewed from the demolition site opposite

89 – A slightly earlier view of the public house, with the Roberts printing works visible on the left

90 – The Kings Arms at the junction of Botolph Street and Calvert Street, with a prominently displayed date on the gable

91 – Lost for ever, the doorway to 40 Botolph Street, a historic building demolished at an early stage during site clearance

92 – The junctions of Botolph Street with Calvert Street and St George's Street are both visible in this view, taken from the forecourt of the Odeon cinema

93 – Southward view down St George's Street, with Sovereign House (extreme left) largely completed - the right hand (west) side of the street was left in a state of partial demolition for many years afterwards

94 – The northern part of St George's Street as it was before clearance, viewed back towards the city centre from outside 125

95 – Looking towards St Augustine's along the northernmost section of Botolph Street, from a point close to the St George's Street junction

96 – North side of Botolph Street 65-69, towards St Augustine's

97 – South side of the street, 54-62 'acquired for redevelopment'

98 - Closer view of a high quality building at 54 Botolph Street

99 – Almost the last to go: 57-59 Botolph Street on the north side *(see also colour photo)* with the multistorey car park in the background

100 – Not long before demolition: 65-69 Botolph Street

101 – The same building when still intact, 63-69 Botolph Street

102 – Rear of 60 Botolph Street

103 – Botolph Street, 60-62, the last building on the south side of the street before arriving at the Pitt Street corner

104 – Westward view beyond the entirely cleared south side of Botolph Street into the rear of the still-standing 81 Pitt Street

105 – Looking back down Pitt Street towards the city centre, 74-86

106 – Loss of another ancient building, the rear of 58 Botolph Street

107 – View across newly-cleared ground towards 76-84 Pitt Street

108 – Looking past the surviving 81 Pitt Street to Gildencroft and the brick tower of St Augustine's Church beyond

109 – A glimpse past 81 Pitt Street towards the as-yet undemolished Odeon cinema

110 - Looking across Pitt Street at 81, with the completed Sovereign House behind *(see also colour photo)*

111 – Shops at 76-84 Pitt Street, viewed towards St Augustine's

112 – The Norvic Social Club at 70-72 Pitt Street

113 – Northward view from outside 70 Pitt Street

114 – The back of 67 Pitt Street, one of a number of what were originally fine residences lining the street before industrialisation *(as cover picture)*

115 – The Singer Sewing Machine Company premises at 64-66 Pitt Street: the viewpoint is about 100 metres north from that of the same street in picture 17 *(see also colour photo)*

116 – The frontage of 67 Pitt Street

117 – Part of the site of George Fowler Printers, 59-65 Pitt Street, after demolition around 1973 *(see also colour photo)*

118 – The facade to 65 Pitt Street a few years before demolition

119 – The doorway to 86 Pitt Street, close to the St Augustine's junction

120 – St Augustine's Church during a 1960s winter

121 – Frank Edwards' warehouse, the westward view from Leonards Street towards the rear of 23-25 St Augustine's Street

122 – The east side of St Augustine's Street, 23-25

123 – Slightly further up the street, 27-33 St Augustine's

124 – The junction of Sussex Street and St Augustine's Street (see also colour photo), from a viewpoint outside 37 St Augustine's Street

125 – The view from the same point, but looking further northward up St Augustine's Street towards Aylsham Road

126 – Stone street plate on the south side of 42 St Augustine's Street

127 – The north side of Sussex Street, 13-15

128 – 19 Sussex Street    129 – 17 Sussex Street    130 – 21 Sussex Street

131 – 19-21 Sussex Street

132 – 27-31 Sussex Street

133 – 29 Sussex Street

134 – 31 Sussex Street

135 – View towards St Augustine's, taking in 1-31 Sussex Street

136 – 37 Sussex Street

137 – 57 Sussex Street

138 - 48-50 St Augustine's

139 – Looking back down St Augustine's towards Sussex Street

140 - The Royal Oak public house, 64-66 St Augustine's

141 – Esdelle Street, viewed towards St Augustine's from its junction with Edward Street

142 – Moving back to Pitt Street, this is the view from St Mary's Alley towards 3 Pitt Street and back down Duke Street

143 – Looking down Pitt Street towards St Crispin's Hall, with the site immediately north of 3 now cleared of buildings

144 – The corner of Muspole Street and Duke Street

145 – The view from Muspole Street 31-33 towards the Pitt Street junction

146 - Hipperson's cycle shop at the junction of Pitt Street with Muspole Street - by 2019 this building has been considerably reworked

147 – Looking down Pitt Street towards the cleared inner ring road area

148 – Pitt Street junction with Muspole Street, looking north

149 – Looking south down Duke Street, 47-61

150 – The double doorway at 57-59

151 – St Mary's Plain viewed towards Pitt Street and Muspole Street

152 - Pickerell's House in Rosemary Lane, viewed northwards

153 – St Mary's Church from outside Pickerell's House

154 – The former Unicorn public house at 39 Oak Street

155 – The view eastward back out of Unicorn Yard behind the pub

156 – Former mansion and later factory building at 24 Coslany Street, with the Red Lion public house on the left

157 – The Barnard's iron foundry building (right) and an adjacent 17th century house, 22 Coslany Street, under demolition

158 – Barnard, Bishop & Barnard Norfolk Ironworks building (where the bridge visible in picture 1 was manufactured) fronting Coslany Street

159 – The view towards St Miles Bridge some years later, after demolition of the original foundry buildings

160 – Rosemary Lane, with Pickerell's House (photo 152) in the distance

161 – 2-4 St Miles Alley

162 – North-eastward view across St Michael's churchyard to 2-4 St Miles Alley

163 – South-eastward view, showing 1 St Miles Alley and (right, on corner) 59 Colegate before renovation and/or rebuilding

164 – 1 St Miles Alley from across Colegate

165 – The view up St Miles Alley showing 59 Colegate

166 – 1 St Miles Alley after demolition of 59 Colegate

167 – From similar viewpoint, 57 Colegate and 34 Duke Street

168 – 59 Colegate, looking towards St Michael's Coslany Church

169 – North-eastwards across the Duke Street/Colegate junction to the Golden Star public house

170 – Duke Street, looking southwards towards the Golden Star

171 – 34 Colegate, at the junction with Duke Street

172 – 52 Colegate, with Norwich Central Youth Hall (a former school) visible across Duke Street

173 – Northwards view from St George's Colegate churchyard wall to the saved block of buildings at 1-9 Muspole Street prior to their renovation

174 – St George's Alley and 1 Muspole Street

175 – The remaining ground floor of a former two-storey house at 8 Muspole Street, with the right hand door formerly leading to Yeast Yard

176 – Viewed westwards from cleared site across road at Alms Lane, former houses at 14-18 Muspole Street

177 – St George's Street looking northwards past 80-82 towards the Heatrae factory and the old Odeon cinema in the distance

178 – St George's Street looking southwards, 80-82 and the remains of 84

179 – From the cleared site between St George's Street and Calvert Street, the rear wing of Bacon House, 31 Colegate

180 – The view eastwards from a large area of cleared ground towards Pope's Buildings and Octagon Chapel

181 – Pope's Buildings and 7-9 Calvert Street prior to their restoration

182 – 7-11 Calvert Street before renovation

183 – The north side of Pope's Buildings, from Calvert Street

184 – A closer view of north side of Pope's Buildings

185 – St George's Street looking southwards towards the bridge, viewed from the Colegate junction

186 – St George's Street looking northwards towards Colegate corner

187 – Bacon House, 31 Colegate, prior to completion of its renovation

188 – Looking into Calvert Street from the junction with Colegate

189 – 25-29 Colegate, viewed westwards towards Calvert Street

190 – From Octagon Chapel forecourt, the view westwards to the rear of 1 Calvert Street, a former house and factory

191 – Standing on the north side of Fishergate, the former Duke of Marlborough public house, 29, with Thoroughfare Yard to the left

192 – The Duke of Marlborough public house after renovation

193 – View of the rear of the Duke of Marlborough, with the access to Thoroughfare Yard in the foreground

St Martin's Lane, 49-51 – *see also photo 9*

St Martin's Lane, 47 and Quaker Lane – *to east (right) of photo 9*

30-32 Calvert Street – *see also photo 37*

15-17 Golden Dog Lane – *see also photo 41*

24-34 Botolph Street – *see also photo 86*

57-59 Botolph Street – *see also photo 99*

81 Pitt Street – *see also photo 110*

64-66 Pitt Street – *see also photo 115*

53 Pitt Street – to south (right) of photo 117

1-21 Sussex Street – *see also photo 124*

The cleared site of 21 Golden Dog Lane looking towards the rear of 40 Magdalen Street – *from just east of photo 41*

A last view Over the Water - Friar's Quay under development

Index

Photograph numbers by street name, compiled from references in captions

Alms Lane, 176
Anchor Yard, 25
Anglia Square, 69, 93, 110
Barrack Street, 59, 60, 61
Blackfriars Street, 57
Botolph Street, 49, 51, 53, 80-92, 95-104, 106
Calvert Street, 25-29, 37, 87, 90, 92, 179-183, 187-190
Cat & Fiddle Yard, 80
Cherry Lane, 21
Colegate, 163-169, 171, 172, 185-188
Coslany Street, 156-159
Cowgate, 62, 69-71
Cross Lane, 36
Duke Street, 142, 144, 149, 150, 167, 169, 170, 172
Elephant Yard, 48, 54
Esdelle Street, 141
Fishergate, 191-193
Flyover, 46, 52, 58, 59, 63
Gildencroft, 108
Golden Dog Lane, 37-41
Hacon's Yard, 73, 74
Howlett's Yard, 84
King's Head Yard, 35
Inner ring road, 46, 52, 55, 56, 58, 59, 63
Ling's Court, 54
Magdalen Street, 42-54, 64-70, 72-79, 82
Muspole Street, 144-146, 148, 173-176
Oak Street, 4, 5, 8, 154, 155
Peacock Street, 57-61, 63
Pitt Street, 11, 13, 16, 17, 103, 104, 107-119, 142, 143, 145-148, 151

Pope's Buildings, 180-184
Rosemary Lane, 152, 153, 160
St Augustine's Street, 17, 95, 111, 120-124, 138-141
St Crispin's Road, 15, 18, 19, 30
St George's Street, 18-25, 30-35, 92-95, 177-179, 185, 186
St Martin's Lane, 6-14
St Mary's Alley, 142
St Mary's Plain, 151
St Miles Alley, 161-166
St Paul's Square, 63
St Saviour's Lane, 44, 56, 57
Station Road, 1, 2, 4, 5
Stump Cross, 49, 51, 64
Sussex Street, 124, 125, 128-137, 139
Unicorn Yard, 154, 155
Whitefriars, 62
Yeast Yard, 175
Zipfel's Court, 79

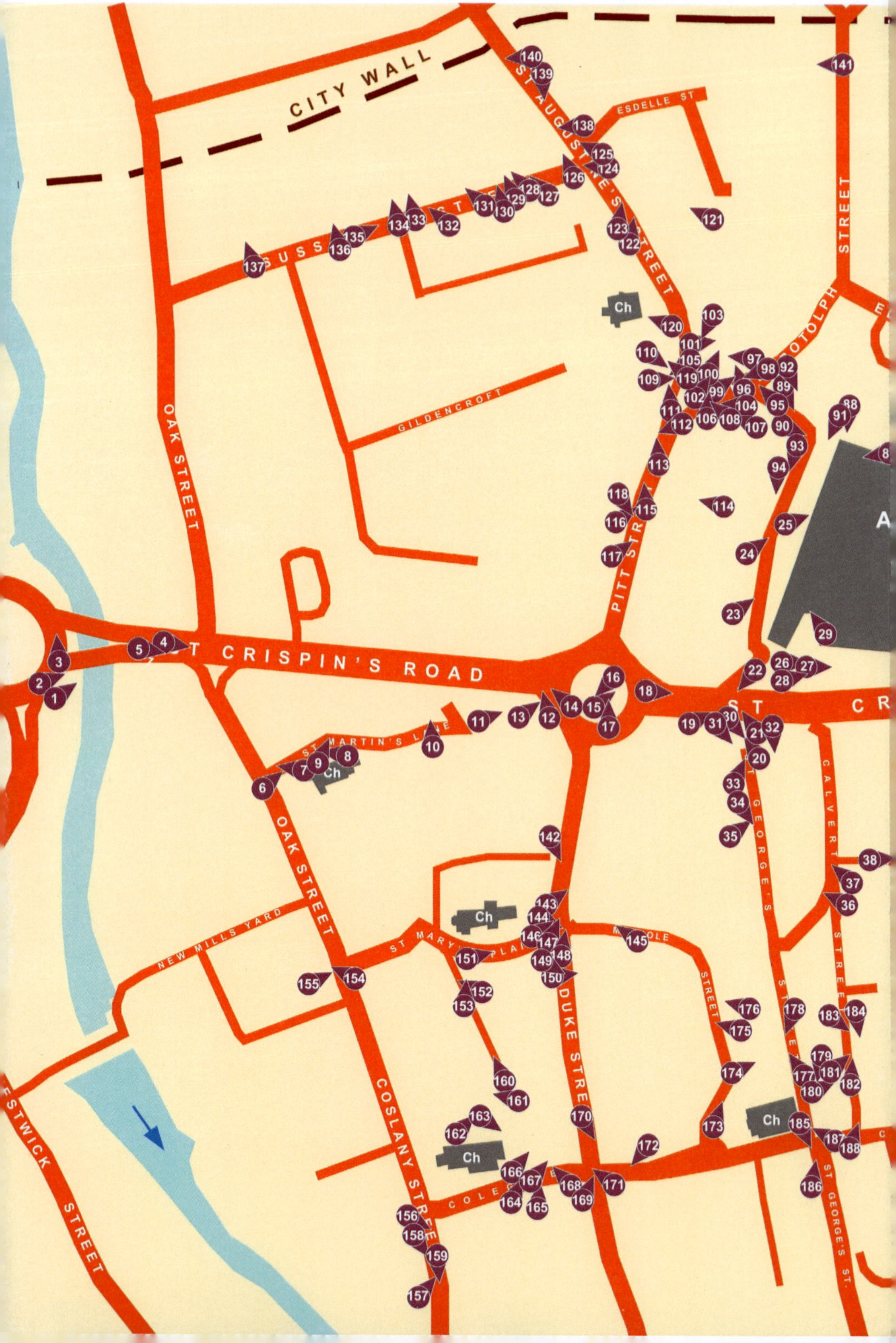
CITY WALL
ESDELLE ST
ST AUGUSTINE'S STREET
OTOLPH
GILDENCROFT
OAK STREET
ST CRISPIN'S ROAD
PITT STREET
ST MARTIN'S LANE
CALVERT STREET
ST GEORGE'S STREET
NEW MILLS YARD
ST MARY'S PLAIN
DUKE STREET
COSLANY STREET
COLEGATE
ST GEORGE'S ST.
Ch